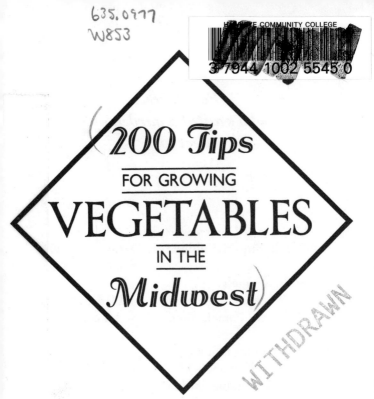

200 Tips
FOR GROWING
VEGETABLES
IN THE
Midwest

Pamela Wolfe

CHICAGO REVIEW PRESS

For Bruce,
who wanted a garden of
sweet corn

Library of Congress
Cataloging-in-Publication Data

Wolfe, Pamela.
    200 tips for growing vegetables in the
Midwest / Pamela Wolfe.   -- 1st ed.
        p.   cm.
    Includes index.
    ISBN 1-55652-175-8 (pbk.) : $6.95
    1. Vegetable gardening--Middle
West. I. Title. II. Title: Two hundred tips
for growing vegetables in the Midwest.
SB321.W77   1993
635'.0977--dc20   92-43359
                                           CIP

First Edition
Published by Chicago Review Press,
Incorporated
814 North Franklin Street
Chicago, Illinois 60610

1 2 3 4 5 6 7 8 9 10
ISBN 1-55652-175-8
Printed in the United States of America

CONTENTS

INTRODUCTION

❧ ❧ ❧

The inclination to grow a vegetable garden begins in the winter. Memories of warm days spent gardening in the sun and the taste of really fresh produce conjure a mental paradise. But once spring arrives, the best intentions get bogged down by disappointment, especially when weeds take over and the soil refuses to yield.

Fortunately, if you know just a few basic techniques, understand the soil, and learn the requirements of the plants you want to grow, raising a vegetable garden in the Midwest is not only possible, but a wonderful and very natural experience. The long, sunny summers, deep mineral soil, and the readily available water make this the real garden spot of the country, and this book is here to help you.

Before you read any further, however, I would like to offer a prefatory tip: make a gardening friend. Gardening may seem like a solitary activity, but sharing experiences improves the garden and the gardener. Comments over the back fence, seeds exchanged, and advice given and received last long after the first hard frost. Some of my best gardens are remembered as produce exchanged and friends made. Some of the best growing advice on these pages came from experienced gardeners sharing their knowledge with me in a friendly, personal way that no amount of research or trail and error can replace.

Finally, I want to particularly thank James E. Schuster, Senior II Educator, Horticulture from the Cooperative Extension Service of the University of Illinois at Urbana-Champaign. He provided the expert technical editing and scientific scrutiny that make me very pleased to share these tips with you. I have worked with Jim for more than twenty years. Whenever I encounter a question I cannot answer, I immediately refer to the extension service in our county. Working with him on this project was fun, and as always, I learned some things!

BEGINNING AT THE GROUND LEVEL

❧ ❧ ❧

Soil

| 1 | The best soil is "good garden loam." With these words everything fertile and productive pops to mind, but what exactly *is* "good garden loam"? Simply stated, loam contains roughly equal parts of sand, silt, and clay. These designations are based on the size of the mineral particles. *Good* garden loam also contains about 5 percent humus or

decayed organic matter. Soil of this composition has a medium texture and, if it has not been compacted, has a loose granular structure. Moist and crumbly like cake, it is friable. In agriculture terms, this soil has "good tilth."

| 2 | **A good crumbly topsoil is the gardener's goal.** In many parts of the Midwest once the topsoil, which is highly organic, is stripped off for construction the clay pan subsoil remains for the unsuspecting gardener. (Clay pan, or hard pan, refers to a layer of clay so dense that it is difficult to penetrate with water or a shovel.) Soils that are predominately clay drain slowly and should be amended with materials to help increase the pore spaces between the particles of soil. When added in sufficient quantities, sand mixed into clay soil improves drainage.

| 3 | **Organic matter improves clay soil.** Two-thirds organic matter to one-third clay makes a friable soil. Most compost that is put

into the garden is not fully decayed. It continues to decay in the ground, releasing valuable nitrogen and phosphorus, and as it continues to decompose, the volume of compost in the soil shrinks. For this reason it may seem impossible to add enough composted leaves and wood chips alone to change the character of true hardpan subsoil.

4 **Amend coarse-textured soils with organic matter.** When they are wet, coarse-textured, sandy soils fall apart easily. Sandy soils hold little or no moisture in reserve. With the water, nutrients also slip through the grains of sand, leaching far from the plant roots. Very coarse-textured, sandy soils do not grow a wide range of vegetables or typical garden plants. Compost will help hold the soil together and slow down the loss of water and nutrients.

5 **When planting, mix as much as one-third organic matter into clay soil to hold water and give plants a steady supply.** Sandy soil loses water and clay soil holds water so tightly that it is often unavailable to plants. Peat moss and composted organic matter help maintain moisture levels in the soil. Materials like peat moss soak up water but also deliver it to plant roots. Organic matter particles change the size and dimension of the air spaces in the soil, and even clay will drain and air out more efficiently.

| 6 | **A large, sharp-grained sand is the best type for amending** |

soil. It tends to compact less than fine sand. Gypsum is often sold to break up clay; it will dissolve into soil and boost the nutrient level of calcium. The ratio of sand to clay is just as critical as the type of sand. Add large quantities to improve the texture of heavy clay soil. To a heavy clay soil mix in two-thirds sand by volume: 8 inches of sand turned into 4 of clay results in 12 inches of amended soil.

| 7 | **For 1 foot of loose soil, till 8 inches of sand together with** |

4 inches of clay. Since much midwestern soil comes from weathered limestone bedrock, lime is present in our soils. If you add less than 8 inches of sand, the resulting mixture may resemble concrete—which is also made from limy clay and sand.

| 8 | Soil prepared in the spring for planting must be dry enough to crumble easily. If the soil is too wet, it dries in hard compacted chunks. Working with soil that is too wet results in cakes of mud on your spade, boots, and trowel. When it dries, this soil forms small bricks of dirt that lack good tilth. These hardened remains leave large desiccating airspaces and create a tough barrier for roots to penetrate. If the soil is wetter than a moist well-rung-out sponge in your hand, stay out of the garden.

| 9 | If it is already late May and your garden hasn't dried out, consider adding amendments such as sand, gypsum, decayed organic matter, or all three to reduce the percentage of clay in the soil (do this as soon as the soil is

friable). Clay or clay loam soil contains more than 30 percent clay particles. To determine whether your soil has too much clay, make a ball the size of a baseball of damp—but not dripping—soil. Stick your thumb into the middle of the ball. If the ball does not fall apart, your soil contains too much clay.

| 10 | **Don't choose an out-of-the-way site for the garden, which may also turn out to be the low spot in the yard.** If the entire property drains slowly, consider raised beds with added or amended topsoil. Raising the level 4 to 12 inches usually increases drainage. Use 2 by 4s, 2 by 6s, 2 by 8s, or 2 by 12s of landscape treated lumber built into squares or rectangles. Cinder blocks, old tires, stones, and concrete work as well.

| 11 | **Fall is the best time of year to till.** Usually the soil is drier and easier to work in the fall, and fall tilling is less likely than spring tilling to result in compacted soil. Turning the soil in the fall also allows earlier

planting in the spring. Spring tilling allows soil subject to erosion to be held in place by the remains of last year's crop.

12 **Repeated rototilling destroys the soil's structure and can lead to compacted soil.** Hard compacted soil usually forms below the rototilled depth, but still affects drainage. Only soils that are predominately sand, and therefore single grained, or soils that contain large quantities of organic matter resist compaction. Rototilling to control weeds may create soils that are blocky and hard.

13 **When the topsoil is thin or the subsoil is very compacted, consider double-digging your garden, which increases the depth of organic matter in the soil and encourages root growth below 8 to 10 inches.** Double-digging basically means amending the soil twice as deeply as you normally do: that is, digging two shovel-depths instead of one. When the subsoil is like a rock, double-digging is difficult, but roots will rapidly grow into the enriched lower soils.

14 | **To double-dig, start at one end of the bed or row and dig out not one but two shovel-depths of soil.** Take the top shovelful of the next spot in line and put it in the bottom of the first hole. Dig the second shovel-depth of the second hole (the subsoil) and mix it with ample quantities of compost and/or composted manure. Put this amended subsoil as the top layer of the first hole. Proceed digging and layering soil along the row. End by using the soil dug from the first hole—topsoil on the bottom and amended subsoil on top.

15 | **Double-digging breaks up hardpan formed from years of tilling at the same depth.** Digging up and amending the lower layer of soil improves the drainage of hard, compacted soils. When the lower level of soil is broken up, water and roots easily grow deeper into the ground. A more vigorous root system produces a healthier plant.

16 For soil low in fertility and poor in texture and structure—poor tilth—add green manure. Green manure consists of crops that are planted and then completely turned under the soil. The crops that grow on poor soil and add fertility are many, but are most often annual ryegrass, red clover, and timothy. Plant green manure crops in the fall and turn them into the ground in late spring or early summer. One grower I know planted corn as a green manure. He planted it in the spring, fertilized it, and turned it under in the fall. Your patience will pay off: in time green manure improves texture, structure, and fertility of the soil.

17 Do not allow grass or leguminous plants sown as cover crops in the fall to go to seed. If they get taller than 6 to 8 inches, mow them. If these green manure crops set seed, they may become a weed problem.

18 A green manure benefits all soil, but will not turn subsoil into topsoil. Two-thirds by volume of compost or compost and sand may be needed to improve soils depleted of their precious resources. A green manure produces compost directly in the garden. The cover crops' roots penetrate the subsoil and decompose as humus. It would take many, even hundreds of years of growing a green manure to completely restore what a bulldozer can remove from a new construction site in hours.

19 After turning in the cover crop or lawn, wait three weeks before planting. Then till the ground again. This allows weed seeds, uncovered by turning the soil, to sprout and be turned into the ground. Also many sprigs of grass grow from the small pieces left by the chopping tiller. Grinding them into the ground again helps finish them off.

Soil Fertility

| 20 | For really outstanding production—fertilize. Mid-

western regard for the benefits of fertilizing dates back to the Indians' practice of putting a fish in the ground with each seed. Although most midwestern soil is fertile enough to grow a satisfactory garden, organic or inorganic fertilizer boosts production—as long as you don't overdo it. For years—my busiest ones—plants and seeds went in, were watered and weeded occasionally, and produced adequately, thanks to fertile midwestern soil.

| 21 | Lack of nitrogen results in a yellowing of leaves and a

slowing of growth. When a plant is in bloom, do not apply high nitrogen fertilizer. The plant may stop flowering and begin to grow vegetatively instead. Tomatoes fertilized with a high nitrogen fertilizer are likely to become enormous green leafy plants and to produce very few flowers and fruits.

22 In order to restore nitrogen, fertilize with commercial products that have a high first number, such as 10-5-4 or 15-0-0. The fertilizer may contain organic dried blood, synthetic organic compounds like urea, inorganic compounds like ammonium sulfate, or other compounds. The plant reads them all as nitrogen compounds and uses them accordingly. Compost and manure also enrich the soil with nitrogen salts. Although the nitrogen concentration is lower in compost and manure, this humus has the advantage of supplying other minor nutrients and improving soil tilth.

23 To avoid burning or drying out plants, compost fresh manures for one year. Putting a moderate layer of fresh compost on in the late fall and allowing it to decompose over the winter is often sufficient. Animal manure is an excellent source of nitrogen as well as of other minor nutrients. Fresh bird, sheep, and cow manures have the most nutrients. Although manure contains an abundance of nitrogen and micronutrients, fresh manure quickly builds to toxic levels in the soil. Having said this, I must add that I and many of my friends have spread a thin layer—about one inch—of fresh rabbit and guinea pig manure without toxic effects. Actually, adding weed seeds may be a bigger problem when applying fresh horse manure to the garden.

| 24 | A plant whose leaves look red or purple may have suffered lower than optimum temperatures or may lack enough phosphorus—a major plant nutrient. Some plants don't take up phosphorus in cold temperatures. The color for phosphorus deficiency will be most pronounced on the back of the leaves along the veins. Simultaneously, a section of the margin will turn brown or yellow with a reddish tinge. A night or two of near-freezing temperatures in the spring may be enough to trigger this response in tender, warm-season crops.

| 25 | Do not use any fertilizer that contains a herbicide. Many lawn fertilizers have

herbicides in them. 2,4-D, a broad leaf herbicide effective against plants like chickweed in the lawn, persists for several weeks. If grass clippings are spread as a mulch in the garden, clippings must not have residual amounts of this or other herbicides earlier applied to the lawn. Many herbicides, certified for home lawn use, lose their toxic effect after several days to several months in the compost pile.

| 26 | **Subsoil is not as fertile as topsoil.** A soil profile, a vertical look at a section of soil, shows these layers clearly. Topsoil is the dark layer rich with decayed organic matter. Subsoil is a lighter under layer. The parent material, which originated from bedrock, is under these. Exhausting the topsoil from years of cropping or removing it during construction creates less productive subsoil, which requires amending.

| 27 | For an established and productive garden, mix in a general purpose 10-10-10 garden fer-

tilizer at the rate of 1 to 1½ pounds for 100 square feet before planting. This restores the nutrients taken out of the soil by the crops during the previous season. Although an organic fertilizer works well, add it in larger amounts because it contains a lower percentage of nitrogen, phosphorus, and potassium.

| 28 | Even without a soil test, a good fertilizer regime incorporates a slow-release garden fertilizer like 10-10-10 or 5-10-5 as the soil is being prepared. This is broadcast over the bed at the rate of 1 pound per 100 square feet before the seeds or plants are put in.

| 29 | A general starter fertilizer (for use at planting time) is high in phosphorus. Those with an analysis such as 9-45-15, 15-30-15, or 10-52-17 are examples of starter fertilizers. Any fertilizer with a middle number that is two to five times the first number qualifies as a starter fertilizer (the middle number represents the amount of phosphorus and the first number the amount of

nitrogen). The higher the ratio the better. These fertilizers stimulate root growth and help the seedlings recover from transplant shock.

| 30 | If plants require additional fertilization during the growing season, either water with a soluble fertilizer or side-dress with a granular one. (Always follow the label for application rates.) To side-dress the fertilizer, spread it evenly at a distance of 4 to 6 inches away from the stem. Putting it any closer may cause fertilizer burn. Although the plant will rapidly take up soluble fertilizers mixed in water, beware the price tags.

| 31 | Side-dressing a fertilizer during the growing season supplements the fertilizer you used at planting time. Read plant signs like yellowing leaves, lack of flowers and fruit, or general decline in vigor to determine the need for fertilizing during the growing season. Look for signs of plant stress, particularly when there has been no initial fertilization of the soil or soil test. Any-

time during the growing season, an organic or inorganic fertilizer—placed about 4 inches from either side of the plant or seed row—boosts plant growth.

32 **Spread fresh manure on your garden as a mulch in the fall to improve your soil's fertility without lowering nitrogen levels as other undecomposed mulches will do.** Keep in mind, however, that fresh manure tends to be physically and chemically "hot" and fresh cow and horse manures usually contain weed seeds. For that reason it is often composted first. Some decay will take place over the winter.

33 **A soluble fertilizer mixed with water will quickly supply nutrients to the plant.** In addition to taking up fertilizer through the roots, plants get a foliar dose with liquid fertilizer. With a liquid, calculating the exact concentration at the time of application results in uniform, balanced growth. Using a constant liquid feed program, plants get the nutrient salts steadily—without fertilizer burn.

34 **Although many municipal waste products are not recommended for vegetable gardens, using sludge on flowers, trees, and shrubs produces no ill effects.** Any heavy metals present do not damage flowers and are not a problem if the plants are not eaten. Composted sludge works well as a source of organic material for ornamental beds. Research is being done to test the feasibility of using all sorts of industrial and municipal organic wastes for growing turf grasses and sod.

Mulch

35 **A 2- to 4-inch layer of mulch helps conserve water during dry summer stretches.** The mulch traps moisture underneath and slows evaporation. When deep crevices form during periods of drought, water evaporates even faster. Mulch slows this evaporation because a layer on the surface of the soil reduces the crusting and cracking soil.

If you prevent these cracks, water will be retained for the plants. A layer of mulch saves weeding time, money, and water.

36 **A mulch insulates the soil against swings in temperature.** The midwestern climate can swing 50 to 60 degrees Fahrenheit in a 24-hour period. A winter night may be 20 degrees Fahrenheit followed by day temperatures close to 70 or even 80 degrees. Particularly in the spring and fall a week of 70 degree weather can be followed by a week at 20 degrees, which affects soil temperature. Soil temperature extremes are moderated by a layer of mulch. The temperature of the soil will cool and warm more slowly under such a blanket.

37 **Weed seeds won't usually sprout under a layer of organic mulch.** Although very vigorous weeds will grow through mulch, most weeds are smothered by mulch. Roots from weeds that do root in this lighter top layer are easier to pull out than those securely anchored in the ground.

38 **Leave grass clippings on the lawn.** Since never more than a third of the grass blade should be cut at any one time, clippings will not smother a lawn. But, if you have waited so long to mow that you essentially have hay, rake or bag lawn clippings and spread them evenly on the garden to a depth of ½ to 1 inch.

39 **Grass clippings put in a thin layer on the garden will dry out in a day or two.** They will thus provide many of the benefits of a mulch but won't turn slimy, as they do in a large pile. I have never noticed nitrogen stress in plants mulched with a thin layer of clippings, but this mulch can increase the annual white grub problem in your garden.

40 **Once spring comes you can cultivate chopped leaves right into the ground or rake them aside to plant the already tilled**

ground. Either way, nutrients from the leaves add nutrients to the soil and improve the texture and structure of the soil.

| 41 | **For crops like tomatoes, cucumbers, and melons, mulch can prevent the rotting that results from the fruit sitting on the ground.** During wet periods or after irrigation, fruit that ripens may rot if left sitting on the ground. A layer of straw or other fibrous material keeps fruit drier and away from disease-causing organisms. The decaying of any material like straw pulls nitrogen out of the soil. When using organic materials like straw, watch for any signs of nitrogen stress.

| 42 | **Some organic and inorganic mulches discourage pests.** In a well-drained garden, sand and gravel usually harbor few organisms. The undersides of boards hide pests that slide along the surface (such as slugs). Just pick off the pests. Any nonabsorbent, sharp-edged mulch impedes slimy organisms that creep along the ground.

Diatomaceous earth, full of the silicon-rich skeletons of ocean organisms, gives the same sharp-edged greeting to these gourmets of the garden.

43 **Mulching with plastic around trailing crops makes a soil-free surface on which fruit can develop.** However after a heavy rain puddles easily form on top of plastic. If the plastic is left in place too long, the continuous waterlogging of the soil underneath can result in compacted soil. To avoid this problem, leave the plastic down only while the fruit matures. Remove the plastic after harvesting the fruit, or at the end of the growing season.

44 **Both black and clear plastic serve as garden mulches.** Black plastic warms the soil and holds down weeds in the early spring. Spread it along the row before planting. Anchor the edges with a layer of soil. I've found brick, stones, or clay pots help hold the ends. In my raised beds, I take coat hangers and bend them like giant hair pins to secure loose sides. To plant into plastic, poke through the surface with a garden trowel and dig just enough to insert a garden transplant.

| 45 | **Plastic mulch warms the soil in early spring.** Clear plastic lets in light and traps certain wavelengths of light as a closed car or a greenhouse does, which unfortunately stimulates weeds to grow (see next tip). Black plastic absorbs light but doesn't transmit it. As the leaves grow over the plastic, the warming effect diminishes. Actually, clear plastic will warm the soil 5 to 10 degrees Fahrenheit higher than black plastic will. Warming the soil with a plastic mulch is particularly beneficial to warm-season crops like cucumbers or squash.

| 46 | **The disadvantage of clear plastic is that weeds sprout under it.** After the soil has warmed, throw a thin layer of organic mulch over the clear plastic to slow the weed problem. Once the soil temperature has warmed enough to grow

warm-season crops and the air temperature has also warmed, you can remove the plastic. Hoe or pull the weeds and then put down another type of mulch.

| 47 | Use plastic mulches very carefully on heavy clay soil. A bed mulched with plastic dries extremely slowly. Water seeps in but doesn't evaporate. Since clay drains sluggishly, plastic traps the water. The structure of soggy soil deteriorates rapidly. Most gardens using plastic should be raised slightly above the surrounding ground. Raising the area from 6 inches to a foot helps air plastic-mulched beds where soil is well drained. But the movement of water is so slow in clay soil that raising a bed as much as 3 feet is the same as not raising it at all.

| 48 | Regardless of the type of mulch you're using, avoid the puddling of water on the soil. Puddling is a result of soil not draining or absorbing water quickly enough, and causes the soil to dry with a smooth surface covered with

cracks. These cracks are a sign of compacted clay soil that has lost the granular structure of good garden soil. (Adding organic matter improves drainage, as does raising the bed.) Work the organic matter into the top 2 to 3 inches, and when you water, avoid flooding the area.

| 49 | **Mulch the garden in late fall after leaves are raked or blown from the yard.** Although locust or ash leaves are unlikely to need further chopping, leaves from large oaks, sycamores, or maples tend to mat down when they are wet and to compost slowly. Mow over leaves before raking them onto the garden. The chopped leaf litter raked directly onto the garden makes a winter mulch that decomposes pretty quickly into organic matter of humus. After mulching for winter, try adding to the bed branches found lying around the yard. The leaves nestle against them and blow around less.

| 50 | A layer of chopped leaves lying on the garden over winter will decompose and nourish the soil, and those leaves still lying on top of the garden in the spring can be tilled or turned into the ground, or raked to the side before planting. If the leaf mold crumbles into humus, work the litter into the top 3 inches of the soil. If leaves are still intact, speed their decay by adding them to the compost pile or compost pit, or add nitrogen fertilizer to the soil. Leaf mold produces organic material, which improves the texture, structure, and fertility of the soil.

Compost

| 51 | Compost piles that are turned regularly, put together with alternating layers of fresh organic matter and soil, and given a balanced fertilizer, decompose more quickly than just a heap of yard waste. A mound of yard waste, unceremoniously piled up, will decay more slowly and have less overall nutrient value at the end. Mulch from either type of pile will

improve the texture, structure, and water-holding capacity of soil. However, the faster the decomposition occurs, the richer in nitrates the mulch will be. Nitrogen compounds wash out of the soil and out of the compost pile rather quickly.

| 52 | **Sprinkling the compost pile speeds decomposition.** The microbes, which act to digest the organic matter, need water to grow. Since soaking the inside of the pile will speed the downward movement of nitrogen compounds, wet down only the outside of the pile. Using excess water to wash soluble salts such as valuable nitrates out of the soil is called leaching. When watering a compost pile, use enough water for the reactions to take place. Excess water results in leaching valuable nutrients out of the soil and slowing decomposition. Keep it just "moist."

| 53 | **Compost should not contain animal parts, fat, or grease.** Although these decay into perfectly acceptable humus, they attract

scavenging wild life in large numbers. Even if they are buried, as in the pit type of composting, foraging animals attracted by the scent will uncover the pile. The resulting mess would be very unappealing and unhealthy to say the least. Any other organic material will provide good material for composting.

54 | **Dog and cat manure should not be composted for a vegetable garden.** These animals can carry diseases transmittable to humans: cat feces can carry toxoplasmosis and dogs can carry various species of worms. Burying pet litter in an area not used for vegetables is fine, but until it is exposed to a hard freeze the soil can hold any disease organism carried by these pets. (Thus after a hard midwestern winter, the decaying manure no longer poses the same potential problems.)

55 | **To provide an inoculum of microorganisms for the speedy decay of a compost pile made of fresh green organic matter, many recommend a shovel of**

soil layered on top. If soil is not available to put onto the pile, previously composted material gives the same dose of microbes. Adding these components is comparable to a cook's adding salt and basil to soup.

| 56 | **Leaves, grass clippings, and other organic debris piled directly into a hole in the ground serve the same purpose as a compost pile and help to amend the soil in that spot.** Dig a hole about 18 inches deep and fill it with fresh or dried organic matter. Mounding it slightly is fine. Cover the top with 2 to 3 inches of soil. A stepping stone on top marks the spot. As the material decays the soil will settle. In six months to a year, plant directly into the spot or harvest the compost.

MAKING A DIFFERENCE

🍂 🍂 🍂

Weeds

57 **Pull weeds every time you walk through your garden.** Taking out weeds in small amounts on a regular basis keeps weeding simple. This attention to detail will pay off with a garden easier to maintain than one left alone until the weeds really take hold.

| 58 | Shallow hoeing controls weeds without disturbing the roots of established plants, and rototilling in midsummer actually limits root growth more than either pulling weeds or hoeing.** Once the vegetable plants are in the peak of growth, their root systems reach out into the garden. Pulling weeds tears at the plant's roots. A light, quick motion of a hoe cuts the weed off at the soil level. Particularly when the soil is dry and the plants may suffer water stress, roots should be left undisturbed.

58 **Shallow hoeing controls weeds without disturbing the roots of established plants, and rototilling in midsummer actually limits root growth more than either pulling weeds or hoeing.** Once the vegetable plants are in the peak of growth, their root systems reach out into the garden. Pulling weeds tears at the plant's roots. A light, quick motion of a hoe cuts the weed off at the soil level. Particularly when the soil is dry and the plants may suffer water stress, roots should be left undisturbed.

59 **As a rule, each hour spent in the garden weeding in the spring is worth two later in the summer.** The moist, soft, spring soils give up the weeds more easily and completely than drier summer soil. Seedling weeds come out faster and in their entirety, but older weeds have a tighter hold. Weed seeds sprout all summer long. Oxalis or wood sorrel is a winter annual, which means it sprouts from seed in the late summer, lives over the winter, and dies in the spring. For this reason, although I personally find spring weeding much more enjoyable than the hot late-summer version, gardening takes year-round attention.

Light

| 60 | **Plant the vegetable garden where it will receive the most light.** Two factors determine the overall quantity of light—intensity and duration. Around June 21, the summer solstice, the angle of the sun is as high above the horizon as it is going to get. The higher the angle, the more intense the light. During this time, the day length ranges from twelve to fifteen hours. Longer days increase total light. If your garden is on the low side in number of hours of exposure, make sure it is positioned for maximum intensity.

| 61 | **Although plants will produce leaves with less light, flower (and hence, fruit) production needs as much light as possible.** Corn, broccoli, peppers, eggplants, tomatoes, cucumbers, squash, and beans must all flower.

Eight to ten hours or more of direct light produces the best crops. Gardens planted near trees or buildings do best with midday light. Position the garden far enough away from buildings or trees to avoid casting a shadow on the garden during the sunniest part of the day, between nine and three.

| 62 | **Try to plant the garden as far away from a tree (or shrub) as the tree is tall.** Trees and shrubs not only shade the garden, but compete with garden plants for water and nutrients. Contrary to popular opinion, trees are not shaped like dumbbells with half of the plant below ground. Nor is a tree characterized by a large taproot shaped like a carrot. Fanning out horizontally, most of the tree's roots are in the top 18 inches of clay soils and 36 inches of sandy soils. Although the bulk of the roots are thick in the soil covered by the tree's canopy, tree roots stretch out hundreds of yards into the surrounding ground.

| 63 | Provide some shade for the vine, or pick ripening fruit. |

Don't put fruit in direct sun to ripen. During hot midsummer the intense rays of the sun may actually "sunburn" some fruits. This is called sunscald. Fruit usually grows under the leaves, but if the leaves don't give protection, a whitish area, sunken and soft, may appear on peppers, tomatoes, and other fruits. These lightened areas on the fruit sometimes rot and turn soft and dark. When a tomato ripens, sometimes a sunburned spot remains white or green.

| 64 | Growing vine crops on a horizontal trellis shades low-growing, cool-season crops like lettuce and spinach. |

Use a minimum of four stakes arranged in a square to form the support. For cucumbers, gourds, or pole beans tie cross-members of thinner stakes or twine across these supports. (Modifications of this form of horizontal trellis are as varied as the imagination.) Consider an A-frame trellis to shade the crops inside. The maximum height is limited by the average length of the vine—usually about 4 or 5 feet. Limit the vine crops to three seeds or seedlings planted on the outside of each support stake.

65 During the hottest days of summer, trellises formed from hollow aluminum poles can heat up and burn succulent growth. When twining plants like cucumber, pole beans, and peas touch these hot pipes, their stems may burn. In cooler, northern areas of the Midwest, the metal may not heat sufficiently to show damage, but in other areas it will. Woody perennial vines that cover the exposed metal with leaves during the cooler spring growing period often prevent such injury. Although very thin string or wire can cut stems, a trellis of string or twine, wood or bamboo, or even thin solid metal wires supports vegetable vine plants more dependably than aluminum does.

66 Pollution and ultraviolet light harm plants. Ozone and sulfur dioxide cause damage in many urban and suburban gardens.

Sunburn or sunscald also disfigures foliage. Ozone damage appears somewhat like sunscald. The affected areas lose color, becoming a grayish white or light tan. The upper leaves, where the ozone settles on the surface, show a mosaic of chlorotic and green tissue. The leaves look as if they were misted with bleach. Since the damage is in an area of actively growing, thinner, and expanding tissue, a thin line around the edge of the leaf often dies first.

| 67 | **A plant stressed by too much or too little light may show signs similar to those of disease, but a diseased leaf looks different from one damaged by environmental factors.** Leaves infected by bacteria may first exhibit circular spots of sunken brown, black, or tan tissue. Stems are often soft, black, even slimy. A fungus leaf spot often has an outside ring, like a halo, around the infection.

Watering

| 68 | Put your vegetable garden close to a water source. |

Some water will be necessary for any midwestern garden. One of the critical times for uniform watering of fruit crops like tomatoes, cucumber, peppers, and squash is when the plants are in flower and are being pollinated. Also as the fruit develops, a consistent supply of water insures large uncracked fruit. For plants whose vegetative parts are harvested — any time during the growth of leaves, bulbs, or roots — water is important.

| 69 | Provide enough water to reach the entire root system. |

One inch of water per week given all at once soaks into good garden loam to a depth of about 8 inches. Any amount less than that will leave the lowest part of the root system dry. Deep watering done less often is more beneficial to the garden than frequent shallow watering. Watering the top few inches, even frequently, encourages only the roots at the top layer to grow. In soil containing lots of clay, water penetrates less deeply. In sandy soil it penetrates more deeply.

| 70 | **After seedlings and transplants are established and growing, water only when needed — not every day or every other day.** On average, actively growing plants use 1 inch of water per week. Usually when plants receive this useful rule-of-thumb amount, healthy crops develop. But if the temperatures are significantly above normal and dry winds batter the garden, more water may need to be added. Monitor the plants and the soil. Check for signs of wilting or particularly soft leaves. Put your hands into the earth to see if the soil beneath the surface is dry.

| 71 | **Shallow, frequent watering encourages blossom-end rot.** A deep watering (1 inch of water) will soak to 6 to 9 inches every 5 to 7 days and produce the best tomatoes. Avoid the temptation to come home from work and give

the plants "a little watering." When we were new to gardening and home ownership, my husband would come home from work and want to water "things." I would give him a glass of ice tea and point at the house. We had a very clean first house!

| 72 | Hot weeks of drought followed by several days of rain create water stress in tomato plants. The plant doesn't adjust quickly. At the blossom-end (opposite the stem) a sunken, black area of soft, rotten tissue often forms. During late summer, when heavy rains are few and far between, blossom-end rot is very common. In the interim, supplement the plant with water and keep it moist with a mulch. To reduce blossom-end rot, don't allow the plant to dry out completely during periods of drought.

| 73 | A rapid uptake of water causes thin-skinned fruit like tomatoes to burst. Since there are no seams, the fruit just cracks anywhere—often in concentric circles near the stem end, sometimes

longitudinally from top to bottom. Picking the fruit before it is fully ripe may prevent this miniexplosion. Fruit that is shaded by leaves seems to crack less. (Perhaps the skin on such fruit is less affected by the light or the loss of water and therefore more able to adjust.) Also a mulch may help the fruit enlarge evenly and, therefore less violently.

| 74 | **Use a rain gauge to keep track of when and how much it rains.** After a rain the local news stations usually report the amount. But unless you live next to the weather station, having a rain gauge is the only way to tell how much water your garden got. Rainfall amounts vary widely over a very short distance. Strange as it sounds, a rain gauge is a fascinating device. Walking out and checking the water collected becomes a ritual binding you, the gardener, to the needs of the soil. It is a conduit to tuning in to the environment.

75 For the best results—particularly when using a sprinkler—water early in the day. Plants use more water during the day so the water won't just sit around on the leaves causing problems. Overhead watering in midday will not necessarily burn plant tissue, but during that time evaporation will be highest. When you water in the late afternoon during humid weather, the water stands on the leaves overnight, which promotes diseases. Fungi and bacteria can grow without light, but need high humidity during warm or cool weather.

76 Keeping water from leaf surfaces late in the day slows the spread of waterborne diseases. With the cooling of evening temperatures, water evaporates more slowly from the leaves. The moisture speeds the spread of a wide range of bacterial and fungal diseases, and high humidity further aggravates the situation. Brown or black spots on the leaves or leaves covered with a white powdery coating are the signs of these diseases.

| 77 | For members of the cucumber family the rule is: **water the soil, not the leaves; do not use overhead sprinklers.** In hot, humid weather, waterborne diseases such as blights, wilts, leaf spots, and mildews all target cucumbers, melons, squashes, and pumpkins. Spacing plants to allow maximum air circulation may retard the growth of these diseases. If the leaves are wet, don't move through the garden brushing against them. This will further spread the disease from plant to plant.

| 78 | Watering with a soaker or trickle-type hose tends to **discourage diseases like black spot and mildew.** Foliage that remains wet, particularly at night, increases the likelihood that the plant will suffer these problems. Nights when the dew is thick and days when the air is humid are hard enough on most garden plants without adding water to the leaves. It's best to water the ground directly.

| 79 | Soaker hoses made of black, porous plastic, which seems to sweat water, avoid wetting the leaves. With this type of hose, only a band of soil roughly 2 feet wide receives water directly. To cover the entire bed, shift the hose periodically during watering. Don't guess how much water your plant is getting. Check the soil, and avoid either wasting water or underwatering plants.

| 80 | If you install an underground automatic watering system, insist that it has zone control and an override feature. The different areas of the garden and yard will not use water at the same rate. Newly installed areas may need more water. In general, a turf area may comfortably go dormant in midsummer while a garden may not. Tailoring the system to your present and future needs prevents waste!

COPING WITH THE CLIMATE

🍃 🍃 🍃

81 Cooler regions of the Midwest raise melons of poor flavor. A warm season crop, melons peak in regions that consistently have days in the eighties or nineties with nights no cooler than the mid-seventies. Also, to produce the best flavor, melons require heavy fertilization with a high phosphate source. Vines that are not vigorously growing won't produce the best tasting melons.

82 The enzymes that cause bitter-tasting cucumbers build up during periods of drought, when nutrients are low, and when there is a sharp rise or fall in temperature. Keep plants evenly watered. A composted mulch around the roots insulates against wide temperature swings and prevents rapid drying. If the leaves have a lace-like green and yellow pattern formed by the color of the veins against the leaf, side-dress plants with a granular fertilizer.

83 Spinach, peas, lettuce, and radishes are cool-season crops. Put them in as early as possible in the spring. If the ground was prepared in the fall, plant them as soon as the ground thaws and is friable—usually in March. Snow may blanket the ground after peas are planted with no ill effects. It's the prolonged freezing and frequent freezing and thawing that kill the seeds where they lie. Prolonged sub-zero temperatures for more than 10 days to 2 weeks do cut into the seed's viability.

84 Avoid planting cool-season crops in June, July, and early August. They do well in early spring and in autumn, but they bolt or falter when it gets hot. When the daytime temperatures are in the eighties or above and the nights don't cool off, lettuce stems shoot up and flower while the leaves remain pale and bitter. Peas turn yellow and attract spider-mites and white flies during hot weather.

85 Cucumbers are grown from hills on the ground or along a trellis with 12 inches between plants. If plants grow along the ground, they take up considerable space in the garden. A trellis uses less space but throws some shade on other plants and makes screening against insects more difficult. Put the trellis on the north side of the garden or position it in such a way as to throw shade on plants that grow better in a slightly cooler spot, such as spinach, peas, mustard greens, lettuce, and brussels sprout.

86 Soil must be at least 50°F before you plant warm-season crops like tomatoes, squash, and cucumbers. When the soil is cooler than this, the roots won't develop and extra days in the ground will not give them any advantage. Roots may start to rot instead of grow. Check the temperature with a thermometer or feel the soil to see if the chill is gone. Even a tomato plant that has flowers or small tomatoes won't significantly outperform a much smaller plant once they are both put into warm soil.

87 To grow extra-large fruit, first plant hybrid seed selectively bred to grow large crops. 'Big Max' is a cultivar name for hybrid seed that produces extra large pumpkins. Give one plant plenty of room—for a pumpkin that might be 25 square feet—an area of 5 feet by 5 feet. Next allow the plant's vegetative machinery to build up nutrients and carbohydrates by picking off the first five or six flowers. Then allow only one to three fruits per vine to develop. Make sure the plant receives generous quantities of water and high phosphorus fertilizer. Don't give toxic amounts.

---

88 **Choosing the best cultivar of tomato or zucchini baffles the beginning gardener.** One way to pick the best plant for your region is to pick the one labeled All-American Selection (AAS). These are plants grown in test gardens over a wide geographic range and scored by independent growers. These plants receive recognition for good performance in a wide range of soil and climatic conditions. They outperformed other newly developed plants in a wide variety of test gardens.

---

89 **Another dependable technique for selecting plants is to send for information published by your Cooperative Extension Service.** Many state universities have a college of agriculture that evaluates plants based on performance in that region. The tomatoes recommended for Kansas are not all the same as those recommended for Missouri. You can obtain these lists by contacting the Cooperative Extension Service office in your county or area.

| 90 | In areas where the soil warms quickly but where droughts prevail, increase the root system of tomatoes by planting the stems deeper. Bury the root ball and the stem up to the top three or four leaves. The stem roots easily in warm soil, increasing the rate of growth. A plant's vigor is always measured by the vitality and extent of its roots.

| 91 | Tomatoes will form roots along their stems, but tomatoes don't grow well in cold ground. To plant early in areas where soil remains cold, dig a shallow trench in line with the row. Soil near the top is the warmest soil and new roots take off faster than in a deeper hole. Put the plant on its side, covering the roots and stem with soil. Bend the leafy top gently up, letting it stick out like a sunbather buried to the neck in sand.

| 92 | **High temperatures retard ripening tomatoes.** Any prolonged period of temperatures above 90 degrees makes tomatoes stay yellow or turn orange. The taste fails to peak, but the fruit will become soft. When the temperatures are very hot, pick any tomatoes that are yellow or pink. Indoors, put them in a shady place on the counter—not in the window. Allowing them to ripen indoors, in a cooler environment (70 to 75 degrees), brings out a better color and taste.

| 93 | **In the Midwest, blossom drop is common in tomatoes.** Watching the flowers drop off disheartens every gardener. Blame it on the weather. Tomatoes won't develop fruit if temperatures are in the mid-nineties—and neither will most peppers and beans. On the other hand, nights with temperatures lower than 55° F won't induce fruit to form. Plants look vigorous enough but refuse to bear, as promising blossoms drop unproductively to the ground. When this happens a change in growing conditions alleviates the problem. Temperatures

ranging from lows in the sixties to highs in the eighties produce the best fruit.

| 94 | **Although blossom drop usually occurs during periods of very hot weather, secondary causes might be involved.** Winds can raise the discomfort factor for plants and make a hot day worse. The plant loses water from its leaves. Wind—especially hot, dry wind—increases evaporation and puts demands on the plant's ability to take up water fast enough. This stress weakens the plant enough to make it an easy target for diseases and insects. Spider mites and aphids may be present under these conditions. Either a change in the weather or a mulch should help.

| 95 | **Stretch the tomato growing season by devising makeshift covers or commercial hot caps so you can put the plants into your garden earlier.** Plastic water jugs with the bottoms cut out or polyethylene cylinders filled with water circle the plant and trap the daytime

heat to ward off the nighttime chill. These protectors help plants endure late spring frosts—very common throughout the Midwest.

| 96 | To protect plants from a light frost in early autumn, water them early in the morning. In the Midwest during the late summer and early fall, several weeks of mild weather usually follow a night or two of light frost. These early frosts often kill only the surface tissue. This damage appears as light, silvery gray patches, which subsequently turn brown or black. If the plants are sprayed when the temperature is above freezing and before the sun comes up, the water reduces the damage.

PLANTING YOUR GARDEN

❦ ❦ ❦

Starting From Seed

97 **Start seeds indoors using pasteurized soil and containers.** Fungal and bacteria spores are everywhere waiting for the right growing conditions. Any place previously touched by growing or once growing plants holds thousands of these unseen agents. Newly planted seeds sown in previously used, unpasteurized soil provide certain targets. Buying pasteurized seed starting mixtures cuts down on contamination. Packaged starting mixes are more expensive but more convenient than home-prepared ones.

98 **Use a fine-textured, loose, growing soil to start seeds.** Finely milled peat moss carries the reputation for naturally inhibiting germinating fungus and bacteria. Commercially milled mixtures of peat moss and vermiculite work very well. Some media have these two mixed with fine milled perlite. Perlite looks like tiny styrofoam pellets that, when mashed, feel crunchy. The perlite grains promote drainage while the peat holds water. This medium strikes a balance. Seeds need a consistent supply of water with enough air circulation to prevent bacteria and fungal growth.

99 **Pasteurizing soil kills most diseases and insects harmful to plants.** Most weed seeds are also destroyed. Remaining are the beneficial organisms that convert complex chemicals to compounds that plants can use. To pasteurize previously used, moist soil, put it in a clay pot and heat it in an oven so that the center of the soil is 160° F for 30 minutes.

100 Unlike pasteurizing containers and soil, sterilizing kills all contaminants. Particularly if you are re-using containers in which plants died of some disease, disinfect the pots, flats, and soil completely. Watering all of the containers, soil, and tools with a solution of nine parts water and one part chlorine bleach sterilizes them. After using chlorine bleach, make sure soil and pots are thoroughly aired to get rid of any residual chlorine.

101 Before starting seeds indoors moisten the soil to the consistency of a saturated sponge. Since some seeds have special temperature and light requirements, plant the seeds according to the directions on the packet. After planting, don't water the seeds. A stream of water washes the seeds into a pile at the edge of the pot. To slow

drying, cover the seeds with something transparent, such as a large
plastic bag, or a piece of ridged clear
plastic, or glass.

| 102 | Covering seed flats with a plastic bag maintains even soil moisture. But as water con-
denses on the bag, open it to let it air.
Otherwise the seeds and seedlings
may rot. Be careful not to let the
plastic touch the little plants as they
sprout. Any new leaves touching or
adhering to the plastic by droplets of
water quickly rot. As the leaves get
larger and the stems longer, prop
open the bag to let in fresh air. This
dries the air slowly. Air circulation
slows the growth of diseases. The
newly forming roots begin now to
compensate for the lack of moisture
in the air. By the time the second set
of leaves appears, the plant should be
out of the bag.

| 103 | When seeds are started in-
doors, the rate of germina-
tion is higher when the soil temperature is slightly warmer than the
air temperature. The difference in

temperature between air and soil tends to cut down on the spread of disease. Putting the trays where light warms the soil tends to create this differential. At night the air cools quickly while the soil releases the captured heat more slowly. In areas of less intense light, heat cables or heating mats warm the soil more reliably.

104 As a rule of thumb, cover seeds one to two times their largest diameter with soil. If planted too deep, seeds won't grow. If planted at the right depth, each seed carries enough food to survive until it hits the light of day. It won't make it if its food runs out. Planted too shallowly, the seed will tend to dry out easily. Some seeds are so small that merely sprinkling them on the soil allows them to fall between the crevices of the soil grains. Light is necessary for some seeds to germinate. When in doubt, follow the directions on the packet.

105 Damping-off is the most common disease of seedlings started indoors. Learn what it looks like and how to prevent it. A fungus that grows in soil water causes this disease, which attacks seedlings as soon as they sprout. The little seedling stands there with only its seed leaves and then falls over — never to get up. The soil is too wet and lacks enough air.

106 Sometimes seedlings with the fungal disease that causes damping-off fall over when they are watered with a spray bottle or watering can, and they don't pop back up. The damping-off fungus grows right below the soil level and girdles the stem of the germinating seedling. To prevent this, use pasteurized soil and sterile containers. Use a soil mixture milled for a balance between water retention and air circulation.

107 To get a head start on the season, plant the seeds in containers, such as peat pots, that will decompose in the ground. Peat pots break down if they are completely buried in soil. If the edge of the pot pokes above the soil, it acts like a wick, allowing water to be drawn out of the ground. When that happens, the pot does not break down and instead becomes a quickly drying barrier between the plant and the surrounding soil. To speed integration with the soil, slit the pot carefully in several spots and tear the top edge back. You don't need much depth of soil, so cutoff milk cartons or liter soda containers, cleaned out egg shells, egg cartons, paper cups, and even plastic bags all work well for starting seedlings.

108 **If you are planting seeds indoors, carefully prepare the soil.** The clean, moist seed-starting mix must be absolutely flat and compressed in the container. If not, the light texture of seed-starting media makes a lumpy surface with air pockets that will dry quickly and kill the seeds. Tamp the soil firmly with a small board, a chunk of wood, or something smooth. Even taking one tray or pot to press down and smooth the soil of another will work. The soil must be even.

109 **Compressed peat pellets work to start seeds.** Put the pellets in a tray with the pellets' small depressions facing up and add water. When watered, the dry, compressed peat moss in the pellets swells like a little sponge. The swollen peat-filled blocks make convenient containers. If both seedlings sprout in the pellet, prick off one of the seedlings. Before planting, carefully remove the nylon netting around the peat ball. The netting, which helped form the pot, may strangle the roots and will be left in the soil for years to come. Plant the peat moss ball and the seedling directly into the soil. Make sure the peat pellet is totally covered with soil.

110 **Saving vegetable seed from your garden for next year's planting usually results in inferior plants.** With many, such as tomatoes, cucumbers, and peppers, the plants you buy are usually hybrids bred for one or more outstanding characteristics. The seeds that result from hybrid plants will not be the same as the parents. They may revert to characteristics of the "grandparents." The hybrid vigor may be lost and so may the disease resistance, size of fruit, habit of plant, and productivity. In some cases seeds from hybrid plants are sterile.

| 111 | **Flowers must be pollinated to produce fruit.** The pollen may come from the same plant or from one nearby. Various plants may be pollinated by different, but closely related, plants. For instance different varieties of melon will cross-pollinate with each other. All sorts of pumpkins and winter squash will cross-pollinate, as will different varieties of cucumbers. The resulting fruit is not affected. Only the seeds carry any genetic information from these crosses. This is another reason not to save seeds from the vegetable plants growing in your garden.

112 If you don't use an entire packet of seeds, the leftovers can probably be used the next year. To keep most vegetable seeds alive over winter, store them in a cool, dry place. Temperature extremes reduce seed viability. Cucumber, tomato, squash, radish, and cabbage seeds usually remain alive or viable for two years or more. For all plants the percentage of viable seeds declines each year. Even when properly stored, parsley, onion, and parsnip have a shorter shelf life and do not last more than one year.

113 Seeds that are soaked and then allowed to dry out die. Once the water penetrates the seed coat, irreversible processes begin. The plant then needs a consistent supply of water. Sprinkling newly planted seeds may kill the seeds. On sunny, windy days water travels by capillary action from one tiny soil pore to the next. The wind draws the water out of the ground. To break this chain, cover the seed with a layer of rich moist compost like bagged cow manure and top that layer with dry soil or organic matter. The dry soil serves as a lid, keeping in the moisture and enabling the seed to begin growing as soon as it is planted.

| 114 | **Thin seedlings after they begin to grow.** Allowing every seed planted to mature results in stunted, spindly, and weak plants. Seeds carefully sprinkled in a row strangle each other unless some are pricked off early. Pulling out or snapping off every other seedling or every two out of three seedlings allows the remaining plants to grow larger. Thinking that a little extra fertilizer and water will support the whole lot, many gardeners grow dwarfed lettuces, radishes, carrots, etc. due simply to a lack of conviction. Rip out a few of them.

115 The following table gives the approximate spacing to which many commonly grown vegetables should be thinned.

Beans 4″

Beets 3″

Broccoli 12″

Cabbage 12″

Carrots 3″

Cauliflower 15″

Chinese Cabbage 12″

Corn 10″

Cucumber 6″ on trellis
5′ hilled

Eggplant 12″

Leaf Lettuce 6″

Muskmelon 6′ hilled

New Zealand Spinach 8″

Onion 3″

Parsley 6″

Pea 3″

Pepper 12″

Potato 12″

Pumpkin 4–8′ hilled

Radish 3″

Spinach 4″

Summer Squash 3′ hilled

Swiss Chard 6″

Tomatoes   30″ in cage
Watermelon   5′ hilled
                     18–24″ staked
                     (small cultivars)
                     3′ if on ground
Winter Squash   6′ hilled

Using Transplants

| 116 | If you want only a few plants of a particular vegetable, consider buying transplants. An entire packet of zucchini seeds produces enough plants to cover an "acre." For leafy plants like lettuce or spinach, the many plants needed are better grown from seeds. Sometimes putting in transplants gives the gardener a jump on the growing season. But if the seed grows fast, often it doesn't matter whether seeds or transplants are put in. Seeds will grow just as quickly as transplants of a warm-season crop that are put into soil that is not yet warmed up.

117 Buying a plant in a very small container for a relatively low price may not be a bargain. A small, matted root ball will not transplant and adapt easily. A plant is most vigorous when its roots just reach the outside of the container and are *beginning* to grow to the bottom. The root tips should be turgid, white, and appear a little fuzzy. These plants will lose the fewest roots during transplanting and blend quickly with the surrounding soil.

118 Many gardeners try to get the largest tomato transplants they can, hoping to have ripe tomatoes as soon as possible, but these large plants actually take longer to adapt to the soil and often grow less vigorously than smaller plants. Plants with pencil-sized stems and dark green color establish more quickly than larger plants. When the weather does turn warm enough, the smaller plants easily catch up with the competition. If you're especially eager to bite into a homegrown tomato, pick early-bearing varieties, but remember: they probably won't taste as good as the later-season plants.

119 **Harden off transplants before planting them in the garden.** Hardening off means gradually subjecting the plants grown in greenhouses, windows, or hotbeds to less water, cooler temperatures at night, and more direct, intense light and wind. If put straight into the garden, seedlings taken from the warm, well-watered, low-light conditions of a gardener's kitchen window will wither quickly. Ease out plants grown indoors by leaving them in the shade near a doorstep for a few hours. Each day increase the hours they are outdoors. After one to two weeks of this they will be hardened off.

120 **Whether using seeds or transplants, water the bed before planting.** A dry bed easily desiccates anything put into it. Moist soil provides an environment into which roots quickly move. Even waiting the minutes or hours it would take to water the bed after planting gives dry soil plenty of time to suck water from tender roots. After planting, transplants need a thorough watering to seal any large airspaces that would dry out roots. Allow the soil time to dry out before walking on or working in the bed. Seeds are better left alone or sprinkled lightly.

| 121 | **Keep newly planted transplants well watered for a day or two after planting.** Since transplanting plants naturally tears off roots, they take up water less effectively. Even plants growing in individual containers lose some root hairs during transplanting. In a healthy plant, roots begin to reform right away. Although extra water helps plants take up needed moisture through the reduced system, the amount is critical. Most roots kept sodden risk rotting.

| 122 | **Like tomato plants, members of the cucurbits—cucumbers, squash, melons, and pumpkins—can be planted slightly deeper in the soil than they were in**

the pot. They will form additional roots along part of the buried stem. When digging the hole, note carefully the difference in temperature between the surface of the soil and the bottom of the hole. Cucurbit roots won't develop in cool soil. As with tomatoes, cucurbits can be planted horizontally in a shallow trench or, when the soil warms a little, deeper and vertically.

| 123 | **For two to three days, shade newly planted transplants from intense sunlight.** Plants put into the ground during hot, sunny days of late spring and early summer lose water quickly. Transplanting any plant tears root hairs and cuts off much of the plant's ability to take up water. Shading the plant from the hot light helps slow the loss of water from the reduced root system until new roots and root hairs grow. Leaves of plants not hardened off will also suffer from sunburn.

| 124 | **Covering newly transplanted seedlings with newspaper protects them from**

intense sunlight. The light-weight cover reduces the sunlight and shelters transplants from strong winds. This slows water loss from plants. Soaking or anchoring the papers down helps keep them from blowing all over the garden. Try inverted pots, rock, or soil along the edges as an anchor. If you water the paper, chances are that by the time wet papers dry, your patience with the technique will be gone. Still, when I've left papers on for even a few hours, the plants recover from transplanting more quickly than uncovered plants do.

Beginning New Beds

| 125 | One method for starting a new bed is to use smothering **mulch.** Using newspaper topped with other amendments improves the soil structure as it stops the growth of any grass or weeds. Some gardeners I know soak an unfolded section of roughly twenty pages of newspaper and then sandwich it between layers of compost. Thick lay-

ers of wet newspaper covered with sand and/or organic matter will decompose enough over the winter and yet will prevent the growth of weeds. In the spring, till this covering into the soil.

126 **One way to kill grass in an area for a new bed is to roto-till the plot over a period of a few weeks.** The first tilling kills most of the grass but exposes ungerminated weed seeds. After this let the ground lie fallow. After about three weeks, new seeds sprout and many of the grass rhizomes begin to grow again. After this second growth spurt begins, rototill the garden. Killing this wave of weed seedlings immediately makes the garden more weed-free.

127 **One method to remove sod from the new garden site is to kill it.** Many materials laid out on the grass will do the trick. Old pieces of carpeting, black plastic, newspaper, pieces of plywood, all serve the function nicely. These must be left in place for more than three weeks to kill the grass. Also, the materials should be laid out in an area slightly larger than the final garden. Sod has the habit of quickly closing in on dead spots.

128 **Corn, winter squash, and watermelons take the largest amounts of garden space.** Since each corn plant produces just one or two ears and nearly 1 foot is needed between plants, only large gardens can afford the necessary space. Also, corn is pollinated by the wind. Each kernel develops from a separate flower. If one flower misses pollination, a gap is left in the ear. At least two rows growing side by side gives better results than does one long row. Planting corn in blocks means planting several rows next to one another and insures better pollination.

129 **Avoid planting a garden near a walnut tree.** Walnut trees have a toxin in their roots that kills or stunts the growth of many plants. When this toxin, jugalone, is present in the soil, plants like tomatoes will be severely stunted or injured and may die. The main concentration of roots is located under the drip-line of the tree. But tree roots spread out easily as far from the tree as the tree is tall. In some cases, plants *much* further away are affected. Only an obstacle such as a foundation, cliff, or road will block the spreading roots.

GROWING HINTS

❧ ❧ ❧

General

130 Interplanting allows two crops with different growth habits to grow close together. When seeds of early and late producing plants are mixed, the harvest of the early crop gives the later maturing plants more room to grow. Radishes and carrots work well together this way. Harvesting the radishes thins the carrots.

| 131 | Plant warm-season crops after earlier cool-season crops are harvested. Rotating crops into the spaces vacated by plants past their peak extends the productivity of the garden. The early radishes, leaf lettuce, green onion, and spinach finish in time to put in beans, cucumbers, corn, and squash. Peas end in June and late cabbage or cauliflower follows easily. Bush beans dwindle in late July to mid-August, giving plenty of time for fall lettuce or spinach.

| 132 | Provide plants with support before they need it. A pea fence put up after the plants are 12 inches tall takes hours. Each plant flops around, going anywhere but up the wire or string. Tying each up or weaving them in and out by hand is not an efficient way to garden. Put the support up when the seeds are planted or shortly after. The tendrils are more likely to cling to the support from the start.

Tomatoes

133 | **Tomatoes are the most widely home-grown vegetable.** Tomatoes are grown in one of three basic ways—in wire cages, staked and pruned, or lying on the ground. Most cultivars available today grow well any of these ways. Some cultivars tend to grow continuously, producing new fruit. These continual vining plants that bear fruit over several weeks, called indeterminate varieties, are used primarily for "fresh eating." Staking and pruning them uses the least amount of garden space. Shorter cultivars that bear fruit all at once, called determinate varieties, are grown by gardeners for canning or freezing. These work best in cages, especially in smaller cages.

Determinant = shorter plants crop "all at once" and plants die off "designed" for canners

Indeterminate = vines that produce "over long time," "designed" for home garden for fresh eating

134 Letting tomatoes grow all over the ground is the easiest initial method—no tying, staking, caging, or pruning that takes up time. However in addition to using a lot of space, the fruit tends to rot with this method. Even before the fruit ripens, it develops soft, rotting spots where it lies. Tomatoes on the ground are easy targets for slugs, cut worms, and many soil diseases like bacterial spot. Putting straw or other dry mulch around for plants and fruit to grow on may help.

135 Staking tomatoes uses the least amount of garden space. Tomatoes that form tall vines rather than more compact plants grow well on 7 to 8 foot stakes which are 1 inch square. During the first couple of weeks after planting, put the tall stakes about 4 inches from the plant. Remove suckers as needed throughout the growing season and tie the stems to the stake with heavy twine, torn strips of cloth, old pantyhose, or other material that will not cut into the vine. Tying the cloth strips in a figure eight wrapped around the stem allows the stem to enlarge easily as the plant grows.

| 136 | To stake a tomato, twist the twine so that it forms a figure eight with the stem in one half, and the stake in the other allows free, non-binding movement. Pick off the shoots that begin to grow at the base of each leaf. Remove the side shoot and force the plant to grow up instead of out. You are removing suckers. A plant that is pruned in this way will produce fruit earlier than will the same cultivar without side shoots.

| 137 | Some gardeners use a form of modified pruning on tomatoes. Instead of taking out every side branch, let two to four side shoots at the bottom of the plant develop before removing suckers. This gives the staked plant more than one main stem and usually increases the number of tomatoes produced. Up to three stems can be tied to one stake. To accommodate the extra leaders, I have seen gardeners use two stakes per plant. The extra

leaves protect the developing tomatoes from sunscald.

138 **When growing tomato plants inside a cage, make sure your hand fits through the spaces in the wire.** Avoid chicken wire. Even the shorter, determinate to-mato varieties grow over the top of the shorter, 3-foot, commercial cages. The larger 4- to 5-foot cylin-ders work best. The weight of vigor-ously growing plants easily pulls the anchoring prongs out of the soil. A fierce summer storm may topple a caged plant. Use one long stake or two very heavy stones to help hold the cages in place.

139 **Removing suckers is not usually done on tomato plants grown in cages.** However, allowing all the shoots at the base of each leaf to grow slows the begin-ning of fruit production. Some gar-deners start the season by taking off suckers that grow early and then letting the later suckers develop. This reduces some of the plant's bulk without undue attention. The excess foliage inside later in the season helps temper hot periods, which slow the production of fruit. Here also extra leaves protect against sun-scald.

Cucumbers

140 **Vining crops in the cucurbit family can be grown on a trellis or along the ground from hills.** A hill is an 8- to 10- inch mound of soil. A few seeds—two or three— are planted around the top. After they sprout the plants are thinned, leaving only one or two. Extra seeds are planted in case all the seeds don't germinate. There is a saying I heard from one expert: "Plant one for me, one for the wildlife, and one for God." The vines trail down from the hill. Using the hill method improves drainage at the base of the plant and makes it easier to discern the base of the plant among the tangle of vines.

141 **Not all flowers will produce fruit. Plants in the cucumber and squash family produce both male and female flowers.** Only female flowers develop into fruit. Usually male flowers grow on the vine first. When conditions are right, female flowers start. Identify the female flower by a pea-size swelling at the base of the flower or an extra thick bulge on the stem of the zucchini flower. In order for this to mature into a cucumber, zucchini, or pumpkin, etc., pollen from the male flower must pollinate it. Bees are the most valuable pollinators in the garden.

Melons

| 142 | **Pick most melons when the stems begin to turn brown or when the blossom ends soften a little.** The fruit should snap off easily. Some melons have tendrils. When the tendril at the melon stem turns totally brown, that signals the melon is ripe. Since the tendril also turns brown when it is damaged, check carefully for any telltale signs of bruising. During very warm weather, melons ripen rapidly. Once the stem begins to turn brown, no more development takes place. The

fruit will soften quickly and rot where it lies.

Corn

143 **If you have room in your garden, the Midwest grows outstanding sweet corn.** Since all the seeds planted at the same time mature at nearly the same time, sow the seeds in two or three plantings. This will extend the season. Time the second planting after the first seedlings measure about 2 inches tall. Don't fill in seeds where plants are missing in a row. The growing seedlings throw too much shade for new seeds to prosper.

144 **If you want to get all your corn planting done at once, you don't have to wait around for the first seedlings to reach 2 inches.** Plant three different varieties in three separate blocks. Pick varieties which mature at different times — about twenty days apart. Plant early, mid-season, and late-season varieties in May. The earliest varieties will be ready in 60 to 70 days, the mid-season ones mature in 80 to 90 days and the late varieties are ready in 100 to 110 days.

145 **Several things prevent ears of sweet corn from fully developing.** Each kernel of corn develops from a separate flower. The flowers are very small and not showy. The silks lead to the base of the female flower. If some flowers on the developing ear don't get pollinated or fertilized, gaps result.

146 **When you grow corn, be aware that dry weather during pollination may inhibit the growth of the pollen tube and the egg will then fail to get fertilized.** This leads to empty spots on the ear. There are insects that feed on corn silks. The cut silks can stop or reduce pollination depending on whether the insect ate the silk before or after pollination. Most midwestern soil has enough potassium, but a potassium deficiency may also prevent corn from fully developing.

CONTAINER GARDENING

❧ ❧ ❧

147 | In areas with very poor soil, in gardens with very limited space, or on apartment balconies and terraces growing in containers is popular. Due to growing in such a confined space the container soil mix must hold water well. Yet because most roots that are kept wet rot, the mix needs to provide good aeration. Good garden loam will not drain quickly enough to give a good balance of air and water. A mix close to one third pasteurized topsoil, one third coarse sand or perlite, and one third peat moss or compost will work.

148 Fertilizing once a week, at the recommended rate, can maintain most container-grown plants. The amount of watering determines the amount and frequency of fertilization. The more often a plant is watered, the more often fertilizer is required. A plant growing rapidly uses more nutrients than a plant growing and taking up water slowly. Before increasing the amount of fertilizer given to a container plant, notice whether the plant is drying out from the hot weather or is in a period of active growth.

149 Avoid using garden soil in containers. The clay present in most soil compacts easily. The tiny particles clump together when heavily watered, forcing out air spaces. These spaces are lost and the soil dries hard as a brick, strangling the roots. Add at least two-thirds peat moss or vermiculite. Some microorganisms in soil cause diseases. In the confined space of a pot and given the stress that applies to a plant, these pests may become serious problems. Disinfect the soil with heat by putting a clay pot full of moist soil in the oven and heating it until the center of the soil ball is 160° F for thirty minutes.

---

150 **Pick containers that are durable.** Although a fiber bushel makes an appealing container, it is short lived. With wet soil, nutrients, and roots, such fiber pots decay rapidly. Wood, clay, and plastic pots work well. Make sure to empty any pot at the end of the season. Wet soil, freezing and thawing, breaks the pots quickly. Dry out a clay or wood pot full of soil then cover it to keep water from collecting in it and breaking it.

---

151 **Decorative pots without drainage holes are unsuitable for direct planting.** Put the plant in a pot with drainage holes and set that container inside the decorative one. Always dump out excess water. If water sits inside a decorative pot, the plant's roots will rot. Place stones on the bottom of the decorative pot to act as a dry well for the plant's pot to sit on. Dump excess water out or it will fester and smell.

Sometimes decorative pots have a rim holding the plant's pot off of the bottom. This can help keep the plant from sitting in water depending on the height of the rim and how heavily the plant is watered. Choosing a small container won't compensate for a lack of drainage. The roots will still die from lack of air.

152 | A pot should have a volume about half the size of the mature plant's volume. A plant that gets as big as a bushel basket should be in a pot the size of half a bushel basket. The plant will stop growing and be stunted if the pot is too small. If a plant reaches a size greater than twice the volume of the pot it is in, transplant that plant to a larger pot or be prepared to have a bonsai.

153 | Choose cultivars of vegetable plants developed especially for container gardening. Bush-type cucumbers and tomatoes produce fruit without the rangy growth habit. Small cultivars in large pots require the least amount of attention. Dwarf tomatoes and

peppers won't produce fruit in pots smaller than one gallon. Larger vegetables like squash need five gallons. Leafy plants like lettuce need 6- to 10-inch pots. Parsley, small herbs, and chives will grow in 4- to 6-inch containers.

---

154 **Plants grown in containers must have adequate drainage.** If the pot in which the plant is growing does not have drainage holes, the plant's roots will drown. Holes on the side rather than on the bottom of the pot prevents the water from getting sealed in. Water is freer to drain away from the pot.

---

155 **Pots used for outdoor nursery production and sales are taller and contain more soil than those sold for house plants.** These are often classified by their soil capacity. A one gallon pot contains approximately one gallon of soil. A five gallon pot contains five gallons of soil.

156 To estimate how much soil mix to buy or make, use the following table.

Pot Size	Volume of Soil Held
4″	1 pint
6″	3 pints
8″	1½ gallons
10″	2½ gallons
12″	3½ gallons
14″	4½ gallons
16″	5½ gallons
20″	6½ gallons

157 Of course roots can grow out of the holes in a pot that is buried in the ground. To keep the roots inside a pot, rotate the pot 360 degrees every once in a while. From time to time—preferably once a week—twist the rim of the pot. If you feel the tension of roots anchoring into the ground, rotate the pot to free the plant from the ground. The roots will form new branches inside the pot.

158 Plants grown in containers wilt quickly. Finding ways to prevent wilting produces healthier plants than any amount of catch-up watering after the fact. After a plant wilts severely, the lower leaves yellow and fall off. Once a plant wilts, it loses the vigor it had before the water stress. The first sign of wilting is a softening of the leaves. To catch the plant before the stress is irreversible, water just as the turgidity lapses. Add peat moss to a commercial potting soil to improve water-holding capacity.

159 **After the growing season is over, dump the soil mixes from container plants onto the garden.** The peat moss, perlite, and vermiculite mixes from these pots become a layer of winter mulch. They are lighter weight and faster draining than most soil and add a layer of insulation to the perennials without becoming matted or hard. Since water drains through them efficiently, they rarely become solid blocks of ice. Take the dead plants out of their pots and compost them before dumping the mixes onto the garden.

MANAGING THE MARAUDERS

❧ ❧ ❧

Diseases and Insects

160 | I have noticed that a vigorously growing plant may become infected with a fungal disease but remain basically healthy. The plant growth keeps the problem in check, and only a few lesions or some streaking appear on the leaves. However, if the weather puts an infected plant in a weakened condition, a disease present in the plant for

a few hours to several years may all of a sudden kill leaves, stems, roots—even the entire plant. Changing the location of plants in the garden—old-fashioned crop rotation—avoids the diseases that build up in the soil and benefits even the smallest garden.

| 161 | Diseases that feed specifically on one group of plants build up in the soil over time. Planting the same type of crop in the same spot every year builds up organisms in the soil that feed off these plants. The infestation level is interrupted by moving crops around. Related crops can share pathogens, so rotate the main groups: the cucurbits (cucumbers and melons), cole (cabbage and broccoli), solanaceous (peppers and tomatoes), legumes (beans and peas), and alliums (onions and leeks) every year or so. Let at least three years pass before a crop comes back to a given area.

| 162 | To identify leaf and fruit spots caused by bacterial or fungal diseases, as opposed to a chemical or physiological problem, look closely at the spots that form on the fruit or leaf. Those of bacteria will often be round and sunken — usually with a different colored halo encircling the point of the infection. A fungal disease likewise has a ring of discolored tissue around the point of infection, but the spots may be oblong or irregularly shaped.

| 163 | Verticillium and fusarium wilt are among the most insidious. The only control is to plant resistant varieties. Symptoms are straightforward. An otherwise healthy, well-watered plant slowly wilts and dies. Leaves turn yellow, then brown, and the plant steadily declines. During cool periods the problem is worse. With fusarium wilt, the lower leaves yellow as the plant wilts. This disease flourishes in warmer weather. Both diseases overwinter in the soil ready to attack the next susceptible plant.

164 Bitter-tasting cucumbers come from plants infected with cucumber mosaic and bacterial wilt. When cucumbers, which should be an even color of deep forest green, are mottled with various shades of green and yellow, from which the disease gets its name, the result is bitter-tasting fruit. The mottled and curled leaves show the effect as well. Start with resistant cultivars and watch for leaf hoppers—light green insects about ¼ inch long that hop from leaf to leaf—as you brush past the plants, because they can spread the disease.

165 Anticipate mildew's attack. In much of the Midwest during mid- to late summer, hot, humid air hangs over the garden. When the days bring this hot, thick air and the nights are cool, dew settles. Spores travel easily through the air, which is thick with water vapor, and settle on the leaves during the night. A heavy morning dew signals the beginning of mildew season with its white coating on the leaves. Then plants' leaves begin to curl and yellow. Squash, pumpkin, gourds, and cucumbers are the primary hosts. The best defense is a good offense. Plant mildew- resistant cultivars. Since breezes blowing through the garden dry the air and help control fungal diseases, encourage good air circulation by avoiding crowding the plants and keeping the weeds down.

| 166 | **Pick melons, cucumbers, squash, and pumpkins late in the morning when the foliage is dry.** The entire cucumber family suffers from various waterborne diseases. Walking along, brushing past damp leaves spreads fungal spores. These spores cause a wide range of blights, leaf spots, and wilts. Heavy dew, wetting the leaves, is typical of late summer mornings. These drops float thousands of spores ready to inoculate nearby plants.

| 167 | **Cucurbits, or the cucumber family, include melons, squash, pumpkins, and gourds.** The striped and spotted cucumber beetles carry bacteria wilt, one of the diseases that plague the entire group. The beetles inoculate each plant they

chew on with the bacteria, which causes the plants to wilt and die. Once the plants show the wilting symptoms, tear out the plants and don't compost them.

---

168 **To protect newly planted seeds and vines from the cucumber beetles, use a screen 3 feet wide by 3 feet long and staked so that it is 3 feet high.** After each hill is planted, screen it. These beetles will actually burrow into the ground and infect the seeds before they sprout. Wait too long and it will be too late. The screening must be a very fine mesh. Choose something like window screening or cheesecloth. Any material with a mesh the size of window screening will work.

---

169 **Since the cucumber beetles overwinter, clean up plants at the end of the season.** The dead vines and other litter provide a good hiding spot for them and for other garden pests. If a beetle or a disease plagued the garden during the summer, avoid a heavy winter mulch of uncomposted material.

Insects and Similar Pests

| 170 | Early planted, short-season crops may outrace the brunt of an attack of the nematodes, since the worms multiply and worsen as the season progresses. (Nematodes are microscopic round worms that cause the plants to fade.) Easy wilting on a windy day, persistent yellowing, and a poor rate of growth may all be symptoms of nematode infestation. Some nematodes cause knotty growths on the roots, indicating that nematodes may be the problem. Planting resistant varieties, improving the soil's drainage, and rotating susceptible crops like tomatoes out of infected areas, all help control them. Since the worms multiply and worsen as the season progresses, many nematodes don't survive freezing cold winters of the north. Usually gardens in areas where the ground freezes solid have fewer nematode problems. Sometimes they come in on the soil with plants started in southern areas and shipped to the north for sale.

171 In addition to verticillium and fusarium wilts, some specially bred varieties of tomatoes resist nematodes. Plants or seeds tagged with the letters VFN after the name are resistant to verticillium, fusarium, and nematodes. If a cultivar is resistant to tobacco mosaic, a less prevalent disease caused by a virus, the tag will include the letter T as well. An example is Celebrity VFNT. Better Boy VFN is resistant to verticillium, fusarium, and nematodes. Roma VF resists verticillium and fusarium.

172 Tomatoes and other fruit can be eaten by slugs. For the first defense against slugs, clean away leafy mulch, which acts as cover. Before an infestation becomes heavy, apply diatomaceous earth or very sharp sand around the base of plants. The band should be about 3 inches wide and encircle the plant. For slugs on food crops, do not use baits.

| 173 | White flies easily cover plants with thin leaves and prominent veins. |

Hibiscus, poinsettia, and tomatoes are favorite hosts, while jade plants, sanseveria, and corn seem to be immune. The flies lay eggs on the underside of leaves. Protected by an egg case, the larvae suck the juice. They metamorphose three days later into new flies. If the infestation isn't too severe, a lure helps control them. They flock to the color yellow. Yellow sticky sheets (available in most hardware stores) staked in the garden act like fly paper to catch them. White flies will generally not kill a plant, but can cause noticeable plant damage.

| 174 | Cutworms are among the most discouraging problems. |

Newly planted transplants of tomatoes, broccoli, cucumbers, squash, or newly emerging corn or bean seedlings suddenly perish as if some garden nemesis came with scissors snipping every new stem just above the soil level. That's the work of cutworms. For those plants that escaped the first wave of attack, cutworms climb the plants and eat holes in the fruit. Protect newly planted crops before an attack — afterwards the plant is dead.

| 175 | Cardboard, paper cup, or tinfoil collars around the base of the plants thwart the cutworms' aggression. On newly sprouting corn or beans this may be impractical. Spreading pesticide baits carefully or applying a pesticide labeled for cutworms around the base of each plant, according to prescribed directions, may be necessary.

| 176 | The squash vine borer brings in a bacterium that causes the base of the plant to rot and the entire plant to wilt. There is no chemical control for the disease. As with the bacteria wilt of cucumbers, which is carried by the striped and spotted cucumber beetles, preventing the disease is worth the trouble. Put a large screen over the plants from the time the seed is put into the ground until both male and females flowers are seen on the vine. After being uncovered, the plant will take

six weeks to wilt. By then you'll have several weeks of harvest.

177 **Squash vine borers are a persistent problem, eating zucchini and other members of the cucurbits from the inside out.** Near the base of the stem, a very tiny hole marks the worm's entrance to the vine. It spends its entire summer eating its way up the stem. Since the worm is tucked tidily away once the borer is inside the plant, spraying insecticides doesn't work. A crochet hook or darning needle can help dig out the borer. Also gently slitting the vine to get the worm out and covering the wounded stem with soil to promote new roots can solve the problem.

178 **White flying moths precede cabbage worms.** The innocent moths busy themselves throughout the garden during midsummer. The cabbage worms are the larvae of these harmless looking moths. The worm chews hungrily on cabbage, cauliflower, broccoli, and brussels sprouts. Similar predators, the cabbage looper or inch worm, and the diamond-back moth, also attack members of the cucumber family. Seeing these in the garden signals the first warning of a problem.

179 **Often the bacteria Bacillus thuringensis proves an effective biological control against cabbage worms, cabbage loopers, and other caterpillars specified by the label.** The bacteria survives in the alkaline stomachs of these and a variety of true caterpillars. The bacteria destroys the caterpillars from the inside. Since bacteria live only in alkaline stomachs they are harmless to any warm-blooded animal. This is a safe, effective control that must be reapplied throughout the growing season. Since you'll never kill every pest, apply the pesticide only when the infestation builds to an unacceptable level. Excessive use can develop resistance in these caterpillars. Do not try and kill them all; instead, kill enough so your crop is edible.

| 180 | Varieties of medium and late corn are susceptible to insects not present earlier in the year. (Earworm is particularly hard on late-season varieties.) Besides labeled insecticides, mineral oil slows the progress of the worms. Carbaryl (Sevin) remains the listed chemical for the problem in home gardens.

| 181 | Members of the cucumber family, which includes squash, melon, and pumpkins, are pollinated by bees. Spraying insecticides in or near the garden around the time bees are actively pollinating the plants often kills bees, which causes the flowers to drop off and no fruit to develop. If done at night when the bees are in their nests, village spraying for mosquitoes may not lower the bee population. Also bees get mites and diseases that can kill them. Pollinating bees are an important asset in the garden.

Pesticides

| 182 | **Misuse of pesticides causes problems.** Since some herbicides act by tying up nutrient transport in the plant, pesticide damage may emulate a fertilizer deficiency. Stunted, curled, or discolored foliage is a common symptom. Sometimes a herbicide may cause only brown spots on the leaf. The pattern of spots from a spray may be more uniform than those of an actual biological infection. If the uniform spacing looks like the leaf was sprayed with brown or tan paint, herbicide damage may be the problem.

| 183 | **When a lawn's broad-leaf herbicide spray drifts into the garden, many plants will be damaged or killed.** Look for the symptoms of distorted, curled, and twisted foliage. Tissue between the veins may die out, resulting in a lacy looking leaf. Although some insects produce similar symptoms, these may be caused by some herbicides.

| 184 | When herbicide injury is the problem, the leaf color will be light brown as the tips die.** The newest growth shows the most damage, and even if the plant isn't killed, it will be slowed down or stunted for several weeks. Small droplets and fumes can drift half a mile or more. A foam formula now available for spot treatments seems less likely to damage surrounding plants.

Garden Herbivores

| 185 | Wild things running and flying through the garden can be both a delight and a dilemma.** One neighbor will buy corn for squirrels to feast on during the winter while another plots all winter to rid the garden of varmints. Before constructing elaborate traps or an electric fence, check with your local game warden or community officials to determine if any restrictions on animals or control methods might apply.

186 To deter rabbits try dusting baby powder around the emerging plants. Reapply the powder after a heavy dew or rain. Regardless, a fresh dose of powder every seven to ten days should discourage rabbits. Keep up the regime until the plant gets too large or old to be of interest to the rabbits.

187 The time and effort needed to foil raccoons and deer make the process of planting, fertilizing, and watering corn seem like nothing. For raccoons, present everywhere when the corn gets ripe, an electric fence made with two wires—one at 6 inches from the ground and one at 12 inches—works best. Have it ready before the corn is. Raccoons feed early when corn is at the white milk stage.

188 If you want to try a plain fence first to keep out raccoons, make it at least 6 feet high with 2 or 2 ½ feet unattached at the top. The weight of the animal will bend it back. When he is knocked off, he may get discouraged.

189 **Some people enclose the entire garden, top and all, in a chain-link or chicken wire fence.** This will effectively box out the pests only if you realize that many dig under fences. Raccoons and woodchucks will dig under a fence. Bury at least a 12-inch length of fencing in the soil. Put 6 inches straight into the ground and 6 inches bent out to form an L underground. After all this, it is not difficult to understand the current popularity of farmer's markets!

190 **To protect against deer, exclusion becomes an art form.** The shortest open fence that will keep deer out without electricity or elaborate barricading is 8 feet. Some deer are even able to jump an 8 foot fence! Contrary to popular opinion, really enterprising deer may jump a solid 5 or 6 foot fence. Besides, a solid fence casts shade. Winding 3-foot chicken wire in a maze throughout the garden keeps out

deer. They aren't very good at
mazes!

191 Place several large (3-foot
by 5-foot) loose cylinders of
chicken wire on their sides in and
around the garden. Such a maze will
usually veer the deer to another path.
This system works for a gardening
friend who has a large garden in the
country. The directing of the deer
toward an alternate route seems to
do the trick. In the Midwest, dis-
couraging deer can be an obsession!

192 A very pungent soap (Dial
works well) puts deer off the
scent! A half bar hung 3 feet from the
ground, every 6 feet around the garden works well. Do not use a soap
with an herbal scent: the deer seem
not to take any notice of it. Soaps
that dissolve quickly don't last long
enough to be effective. If any bar in
the chain surrounding the garden is
lost, deer quickly find the opening
and enter there. The soap system
must be tightly monitored.

193 I've heard hanging human hair in pantyhose holds deer at bay for a little while, as do some commercial repellents. Hair and many repellents work until the material oxidizes. Then the scent is lost. (On warm days this can take less than 12 hours.) You'd have to have access to lots of hair for this technique to work for long! And needless to say, it reduces the beauty of your garden.

194 After pollination occurs, try protecting corn from squirrels and deer by tying a piece of old pantyhose over the ear. Cut each leg into two cylinders to cover four ears. The seat can cover two ears on adjacent and closely planted stalks. Tie the open ends with a knot to make a hose baggy over the corn. Although this thwarts squirrels and deer, raccoons may rip off any protective covering to secure the tasty prize.

195 If used according to the label directions, commercial repellents are a useful tool in the ongoing struggle to keep deer out of the midwestern garden. Soak rags with these liquids and hang the rags in the garden at about 3 to 4 feet. (At the level of the plants you are protecting!) As the scent wears off, the repellent must be reapplied. Place rags at intervals no greater than 6 feet. Where any repellent spills on the ground, plants die back.

| 196 | The simplicity of the Minnesota Zaps electric fence is elegant. One line of electric wire 4 feet high surrounds the garden. Every 3 to 4 feet, a piece of aluminum foil folded over the wire hides a smelly, thick smear of peanut butter. Cloth tape on the inside of the foil holds the bait in place. When lured to the spot by the smell of peanut butter, the deer gets just enough of a shock to be discouraged from trying it again.

| 197 | A typical electric deer fence has electric wires that are held out from fence by insulators. The seven-wire slant fence has wires

at roughly 1-foot intervals along a fence that angles out from the garden at 45 degrees.

| 198 | Another inventive system for an electric fence uses two short fences to form a type of barricade.** One fence is 4 feet tall with two wires—one 6 inches from the bottom, which keeps smaller animals out, and one near the top. The second fence, placed 4 feet in front of the first fence, is 2½ feet tall with an electric wire at the top.

CHILDREN AND GARDENING

🍒 🍒 🍒

199 | **A few simple techniques involve children in gardening.** Even as toddlers, my girls delighted in searching the vines for peas, opening them on the spot, and eating them raw. After following you around the garden, children will have their own ideas. When the time comes, let your child pick the area for his or her own garden. Children usually know where they want it to be. If you have several raised beds, turning one over to your youngster makes site selection easy.

200 Once your child's garden spot is ready, encourage some easy standards but let him or her choose from a catalog or garden center what to put in it. I've always been surprised what my daughters could grow! Help children care for their garden. Don't turn them loose with the weeding and watering only to criticize later when the garden turns into a mess. Keep it a positive experience. All of us look forward to our next spring and another chance at perfection.

INDEX

❦ ❦ ❦

Please note: the numbers below refer to the tips, not the book's pages.